Primary Sources of Westward Expansion

The Transcontinental Railroad

Budd Bailey

Cavendish Square

New York

Published in 2018 by Cavendish Square Publishing, LLC
243 5th Avenue, Suite 136, New York, NY 10016

Library of Congress Cataloging-in-Publication Data

Names: Bailey, Budd, 1955- author.
Title: The Transcontinental Railroad / Budd Bailey.
Description: New York : Cavendish Square Publishing, 2018. | Series: Primary sources of westward expansion | Includes bibliographical references and index.
Identifiers: LCCN 2016047021 (print) | LCCN 2016048247 (ebook) | ISBN 9781502626424 (library bound) | ISBN 9781502626363 (E-book)
Subjects: LCSH: Pacific railroads. | United States--Territorial expansion.
Classification: LCC TF25.P23 B35 2017 (print) | LCC TF25.P23 (ebook) | DDC 385.0978/09034--dc23
LC record available at https://lccn.loc.gov/2016047021

Editorial Director: David McNamara
Editor: Fletcher Doyle
Copy Editor: Nathan Heidelberger
Associate Art Director: Amy Greenan
Designer: Raúl Rodriguez
Production Coordinator: Karol Szymczuk
Photo Research: J8 Media

Printed in the United States of America

CONTENTS

Uniting the Country

The year year was 1859, and Abraham Lincoln was in Council Bluffs, Iowa, a town located across the Missouri River from Omaha, Nebraska. He was visiting on business. Lincoln came to take a look at some land in Council Bluffs that had been offered as security for a loan of $3,000 to an associate. He gave a speech on slavery and found himself on the cliffs that overlooked the Missouri River. Beyond the waterway was Omaha, and all of Nebraska and the West.

Someone mentioned that one day a railroad would cross the Missouri and head west. Lincoln is reported to have said, "Not one, but many railroads will someday center here."

Later that day, Lincoln was introduced to a man named Grenville Dodge, a young engineer who had recently **surveyed** the land in Nebraska. Dodge was said to be an expert on railroads. Lincoln soon started questioning Dodge fully. Dodge said later that Lincoln "soon drew from me

The Lincoln Monument in Council Bluffs, Iowa, marks the spot where Abraham Lincoln said, in 1859, that the city would become a railroad center.

Grenville Dodge played a key role in building the transcontinental railroad.

all I knew of the country west, and the results of my **reconnaissances**."

By 1860, the Republican **platform** for the presidential election included full support for the idea that a railroad should be built from the Midwest to the Pacific Ocean, thus connecting the entire nation. Lincoln was the Republican candidate for president that year.

Lincoln won the election, and he became president in

1861. He and Dodge met in the White House a few weeks after Lincoln took the oath of office. In this meeting, trains were not the primary subject of conversation. The South had started to **secede** from the Union, and the Civil War was about to begin. Dodge said that Lincoln told him, "I shall bring the country out safe."

However, Lincoln kept the idea of a transcontinental railroad in his thoughts, saying the idea was "imperatively demanded in the interests of the whole country." He signed a bill in 1862 that authorized construction of the massive project. Lincoln never lived to see it completed, or even fully started, but eventually it was built. One of the people most responsible for that was Dodge. After serving in the Union army with distinction in the Civil War, Dodge became the chief engineer for construction of the eastern part of the project.

The railroad that eventually went from Omaha to Sacramento, California, was a huge undertaking. It overcame all sorts of obstacles—rugged geography, funding problems, manpower shortages, battles with Native Americans, labor shortages and strikes, corruption—it's an endless list. It was completed, and it changed the nation's thinking the moment the last spike connecting the two rail lines was driven. Soon, someone could get on a train in San Francisco and get off in New York, without leaving sight of the tracks.

Abraham Lincoln remains best known as the man who "saved the Union" by winning the Civil War. But he also united the country by supporting a construction project that brought us closer together. That's why we're still studying it today.

CHAPTER ONE

From One End to the Other

In the year 1800, people didn't have much of an idea of what the United States of America would look like in the years to come. There were only sixteen states. America had started with the original thirteen colonies, closely packed along the coastline of the Atlantic Ocean. Vermont joined the Union in 1791, and was soon followed by the first two states to be located away from the Atlantic Ocean—Kentucky and Tennessee. Non–Native American people lived between the Appalachian Mountains and the Mississippi River, but there weren't many of them. Beyond that was open space—lots of it. People knew that there was a West Coast to North America, and that people lived there, too. But Native Americans were about the only people who had seen much of the land in between.

There was no law that said the United States of America had to expand "from sea to shining sea." France owned a huge piece of land in the middle of the country, having just acquired it from Spain. That made the United States nervous, since France—under its ruler, Napoléon Bonaparte—was acting aggressively toward other nations. The French, though, had plenty to worry about in Europe, and the thought of trying to defend its new property in the Western Hemisphere was daunting. It also would be expensive.

The American flag is raised over New Orleans in 1804 after the US completed the Louisiana Purchase with France.

In 1803, President Thomas Jefferson told his ambassador to France, Robert Livingston, to find out if there was a way for the United States to acquire New Orleans, the gateway to the entire Mississippi River system, from Napoléon. Livingston was surprised when the French said they were willing to sell all of the Louisiana Territory to the Americans. The two sides agreed on a price of $15 million, and the details were wrapped up within the calendar year. After the sale was completed, Jefferson said:

> I know that the acquisition of Louisiana has been disapproved by some … that the enlargement of our territory would endanger its union. But … the larger our association, the less will it be shaken by local passions; and in any view, is it not better that the opposite bank of the Mississippi should be settled by our own

The United States took a huge step forward in its growth when it bought 828,000 square miles (2.1 million square kilometers) of land from France. This map shows the lands of the westward expansion and when they were acquired.

brethren and children, than by strangers of another family?

Thus, with the stroke of a pen, America had about doubled its size. It would be like the United States buying Canada today. The United States became the owner of a large portion of the land west of the Mississippi, going as far west as what we know today as Montana, Wyoming, Colorado, and Oklahoma.

North America was changed drastically. It now would be settled more or less from East to West. The continent wouldn't be broken into small nations, like Europe or South America. The major European powers of the day—England, France, and Spain—soon would have less interest in trying to hold on to the parts of their empires in most of North America. That would make further expansion of the United States almost inevitable. In the meantime, America's borders became that much more secure, with so much land and water serving as a **buffer** between it and other countries.

The transaction also meant that America's future figured to be bright. It seemed only a matter of time before the United States would become a great, powerful nation. The United States now had a huge and diverse list of resources at its disposal, with plenty of room to grow. The nation had the chance to be much more than a group of people banding together to try an experiment in democracy. America had a chance to become a major player in the world.

Examining the Purchase

Jefferson obviously liked the purchase. Like any new owner, he wanted to see what he had just bought. The Louisiana Territory was, by the standards of Americans, generally unexplored territory. Few maps of it had been drawn. Jefferson knew that the Mississippi and Missouri Rivers and their **tributaries** drained a vast amount of land. But that land was a mystery. In particular, Jefferson hoped that the Missouri somehow connected to the Columbia River system in the Northwest.

He sent his personal secretary, Meriwether Lewis, on a mission to find out if it did. Lewis enlisted the aid of William Clark, a noted outdoorsman. They recruited twenty-seven unmarried soldiers and hired some workers, and in 1804, they headed down the Ohio River, and then to the Mississippi and Missouri Rivers. The area between central North Dakota and what is now Portland, Oregon, was completely unknown.

Lewis and Clark's exploration of that territory became one of the great adventures in American history. What became known as the Corps of Discovery headed up the Missouri to North Dakota, where they built Fort Mandan and wintered. In the spring of 1805, the traveling party went deeper into the Rockies to the source of the Missouri River. They climbed up one side of the Continental Divide, supplies in hand, and reached a mountaintop. There they looked west, expecting to see rivers flowing away from them. Instead they saw more mountains—mountains that seemed to stretch into the horizon.

With the help of some Native Americans, Lewis and Clark continued to explore the West. Eventually, they did find the Columbia River system, and it led them swiftly to the Pacific Ocean. They described the site of the Columbia estuary in their journal this way:

> Great joy in camp we are in view of the Ocian … this great Pacific Octean which we been so long anxious to See and the roreing or noise made by the waves brakeing on the rockey Shores (as I suppose) may be heard distictly.

Lewis and Clark headed home after a tough winter in Oregon, arriving in Missouri in September 1806. Sergeant John Orday of the exploration group wrote about the reception in St. Charles: "The people of the Town gathered on the bank and could hardly believe that it was us for they had heard and had believed that we were all dead and were forgotton." The traveling party brought back maps, samples of plant and animal life encountered along the way, and stories of contacting Native Americans who had been the only humans to live on this land for many generations.

Lewis and Clark's expedition, depicted here in the Columbia River area, went from the Mississippi River to the Pacific.

Oregon played a role in another step in the development of the West—the discovery

The Oregon Trail

Little known fact: Lewis and Clark left United States territory during their trip.

The Louisiana Purchase covered land that went to the Rockies and the Continental Divide. Lewis and Clark went well past that, heading down the Columbia River to the Pacific Ocean. But which country owned that land? No one was sure.

Spain had explored the Pacific coast from its position in the southwest part of North America. However, Spain's influence in North America began to decline after the Revolutionary War. Russia had explored the area from its position in Alaska, but didn't have much of a claim.

At that point Canada was part of the British Empire, and the English did have an interest in the region. So the discussion came down to America and England. They essentially agreed that since there weren't many people in that part of the world, both sides could occupy the region freely. Residents had few problems living together.

The Oregon Trail changed the situation. Americans were making the long journey from the East in growing numbers, and many of them were settling in the Oregon Territory. That land area also included what we now call Idaho and Washington in the United States and part of British Columbia in Canada. In 1846, the Americans and British drew a dividing line on the 49th parallel from the Rockies to the Pacific Ocean. Without that agreement, American history may have changed direction.

The Oregon Trail became a popular way to move to the West. Some travelers stayed in the Northwest, and others headed south to California. Oregon became a state in 1859, and Washington and Idaho followed it. The extra population convinced political leaders that a stronger connection to the rest of the country was needed.

The path of the future transcontinental railroad more or less followed the route of the Oregon Trail from Nebraska to Wyoming, where it split to go in a different direction.

Chimney Rock in Nebraska was an important landmark for those traveling to the West on the Oregon Trail.

of a relatively easy east–west route. John Jacob Astor, the richest man in America early in the nineteenth century, set up a trading post in Oregon in 1812. It was such an isolated place that no one even knew that the War of 1812 with Great Britain had started. The business struggled, and Astor's employee Robert Stuart headed east on foot to get help for the camp.

The camp was sold to a British trading outfit, but Stuart—not knowing any better—kept going. Not only did he reach St. Louis, but he discovered a relatively easy route to cross half the continent along the way. It came to be known as the Oregon Trail. The path was relatively flat, which made travel in wagons possible. **Emigrants** headed west on that route to go to Oregon, and then in some cases went on to California. The numbers were a relative trickle, and for the most part they had few problems with the Native Americans encountered along the way. The travelers traded goods with the Natives and received guidance while crossing difficult areas.

Thumbs Down

Other explorers soon headed west to see what else the land offered, but their reports were not filled with enthusiasm. US Army officer Zebulon Pike traveled to what is now Colorado. Pike reported that "this area in time might become as celebrated as the African deserts." He was later recognized for his explorations when a mountain in the Rockies, Pikes Peak, was named after him.

A few pioneers and traders worked their way into the northwest part of the territory between Stuart's 1812 trip and 1830. Around that time, economic fate changed the course of events in America. The economy crashed in 1825, and again in 1837. Many Americans had little to lose by leaving the East and heading to places where land was available for free and opportunities were endless. Many did so, organizing wagon

An artist's depiction of the view that explorer Zebulon Pike had when he reached the foothills of the Rocky Mountains.

trains that crossed the **Great Plains** and the Rockies for the Northwest. The route quickly became more crowded.

Traveling across the country in a wagon wasn't easy. It took five months to cross the continent. Much could go wrong along the way—supplies could run out, weather could not cooperate, and battles with Native Americans were at least possible. What was needed was a better and faster mode of transportation to cross the country. One appeared to be on the way.

Taking to the Rails

Roads of wooden rail existed in Germany in 1550, serving as something of a superhighway of the times. Travelers rode above the dirt, providing a smoother, quicker trip for horse-drawn wagons and other vehicles. It took more than two hundred years for the next development in mass transit to come along—a change from wood to iron rails. That made travel easier, as the iron rails were more durable.

In 1803, the same year as the Louisiana Purchase, work began on the invention of a steam-powered vehicle that could replace horse-driven carts. Great Britain had huge deposits

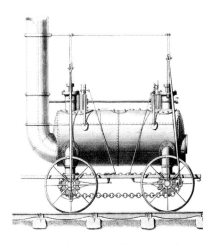

An early design of a railroad engine by George Stephenson.

of coal and iron, resources that helped it start the **Industrial Revolution**. Britain needed more efficient ways to transport these minerals from the mines. In 1804, a locomotive pulled 10 tons (9 metric tons) of iron 9 miles (14.5 kilometers) in Wales. By 1814, George Stephenson had built an engine that pulled eight coal wagons loaded with 30 tons (27 metric tons) of coal up a hill for 450 feet (137 meters), reaching a speed of 4 miles per hour (6.4 kilometers per hour). It was the most successful steam engine ever constructed. In 1825, the first passenger train made its maiden trip, carrying 450 people. Even Stephenson could see the future at that point. His coworker John Dixon was quoted as saying in Samuel Smiles's book *The Life of George Stephenson*:

> George Stephenson told me as a young man that railways will supersede almost all other methods of conveyance in this country—when mail-coaches will go by railway, and railroads will become the great highway for the king and all his subjects. I know there are great and almost insurmountable difficulties to be encountered; but what I have said will come to pass as sure as you live.

Competing with Canals

Train travel soon spread to the United States. In 1827, businessmen in Baltimore, Maryland, were worried they would lose shipping business to canal systems in such places as Philadelphia and New York. They started the Baltimore and Ohio Railroad in 1830 in response, and it succeeded. The B&O was America's first railroad company.

Other new train companies quickly followed throughout the East. Rivers and canals served as the primary transportation method to move freight, but they weren't well designed to transport people. Railroads did a better job at that, and they started to take charge of the transportation industry throughout the eastern half of the country. The total length of railroad tracks climbed past 3,000 miles (4,828 km) and passed canal routes early in the 1840s, and tracks were laid west of the Appalachian Mountains around that time. Still, there were only small railroad companies then, and they couldn't agree on how wide the tracks should be.

There was one more piece of the puzzle that needed to fall in place for railroads to spread across the country. Mexico owned much of the land in what is now the Southwest portion of the United States, but it had never fought a "modern" army. The United States saw an opportunity to add to its empire when it annexed Texas in 1845, nine years after that area gained independence from Mexico. The annexation hurt relations between the United States and Mexico, and the two countries went to war in 1846.

At the conclusion of the war, in 1848, Mexico ceded to the United States territory that included what is now California, New Mexico, Utah, Nevada, and Arizona, and portions of a few other states. Many in the United States claimed that the county's **manifest destiny** was to extend its borders fully across the continent from the Atlantic to the Pacific Oceans, and now the country had done so.

Now that the United States had spread to the West Coast, it needed people to move there. A discovery at John Sutter's mill near Sacramento gave people reason to do so. Gold was discovered there, and President James Polk told the nation about it during his State of the Union address in December

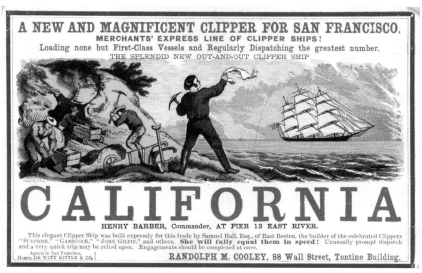

This poster advertises berths on boats that would sail from the East Coast of the United States around South America to California.

1848. That prompted a "gold rush" to California in 1849. Many people thought they could become wealthy there—if only they could get to that part of the world. Some made the trip, and a few became rich. Many of them discovered they liked California and stayed there.

However, getting to California from the East Coast was difficult. It was an 18,000-mile (29,000 km) trip around the tip of South America by boat. Another alternative was to take a ship to Panama, cross that rugged land, and take another boat to California. It sounded easy to consider building a railroad that could unite the various portions of the country. However, other forces delayed that concept for more than a decade.

Overcoming Obstacles

T he first railroad companies started to pop up in the United States early in the 1830s. When they enjoyed financial success, it couldn't have taken long for people to believe that the business could thrive in just about any part of the country. That included the area west of the Mississippi, eventually.

Such expansion would be difficult. The West was complete wilderness. All of the materials involved would have to be transported to the construction sites. That included food and sleeping accommodations for the workers, raw materials, etc. So it would take some time to figure out the logistics, once a route was picked.

The conversation about constructing such a railroad in the mid-1840s was led at times by Asa Whitney, a businessman whose relative Eli had invented the cotton gin, which revolutionized textile production. Asa Whitney had left New York due to personal and business losses and went all the way to China. After a successful stay of eighteen months, Whitney

The Orange and Alexandria Railroad yard in Virginia was typical of those in the 1860s, busy and on the messy side.

returned to the United States with the belief that a railroad across America could serve as a bridge between Asia and Europe and would be of great benefit to the United States. In a letter to Congress dated January 28, 1845, he wrote:

> Such easy and rapid communication, with such facilities for exchanging the different products of the different parts, would bring all our immensely wide-spread population together as one vast city; the moral and social effects of which must harmonize all together as one family, with but one interest—the general good of all.

To be fair, there probably was some money to be made along the way as well.

Whitney's plan in 1845 called for the creation of 60-mile (96 k) strips of land from Lake Michigan to the Pacific Ocean. Lots would be sold to settlers along the way, thus paying for construction of the railroad. When one strip was done, the next one would begin. The proposal was introduced to Congress by Congressman Zadock Pratt of New York.

Others weren't so sure any railroad was a good idea. Senator Daniel Webster of Massachusetts said in 1847, "We want no extension of territory, we want no accession of new States. The country is already large enough."

The proposed legislation was stalled for the next several years. A House committee proposed

Asa Whitney was an early advocate for a transcontinental railroad.

that the federal government act on the idea in 1851, but the idea was buried. Congress had other things on its mind.

Slavery Issue Dominates

Throughout American history, slavery had overshadowed most national issues. During the Revolutionary War era, the Northern states and Southern states essentially agreed to disagree on the subject while worrying about securing independence from England. Some of the nation's founding fathers spoke about their belief to come to some sort of agreement, but neither side would move from its position. Many Northerners thought the idea of slavery was a moral outrage, while most Southerners pointed out that the economy of their region depended on it.

Little happened on the railroad issue until the West began to be settled, and discussions started about how those territories would handle the issue of slavery. **Abolitionists** could tolerate slavery in the South temporarily, since the federal government could not change the situation. But they did not want to see the institution expand into the West. A plan was proposed to let the potential new states vote on becoming slave or non-slave states, but even that "democratic"

approach fell short when abolitionists objected to any spread of slavery.

In 1850, Senator Henry Clay of Kentucky proposed a compromise. California would be granted statehood as a non-slave state, while a "Fugitive Slave Law" that took away most of the rights of slaves who had fled their original homes would also be passed. It satisfied much of the North and South. The

Senator Henry Clay of Kentucky played a key role in events leading up to the Civil War.

portions of the proposal were approved.

But it didn't take long for the issue to come up again, and it left Congress in a stalemate. As Kansas and Nebraska sought statehood, the arguments began again. One of the casualties of the discussion was the Whig political party; it was essentially replaced by the new Republican Party, which held a strong anti-expansion view about slavery.

At the same time, railroad expansion was still under consideration in the 1850s, even if a cross-country line was still almost beyond imagination. The nation's longest railroad in 1851 only went from Dunkirk, New York, on Lake Erie, to Jersey City, New Jersey—447 miles (720 km). The Pacific Railroad Survey Act was passed in 1853 to examine possible routes west. Secretary of War Jefferson Davis (who went on to become president of the Confederate States of America during the Civil War) sent troops to look for the possible routes.

Three Routes Proposed

The conversation essentially came down to three possible choices. The first started with Whitney's concept, heading from Chicago—growing fast in the Midwest—possibly along the Oregon Trail, and finishing in the Northwest portion of the country. The problem was that that route crossed the Rockies through Wyoming and Idaho. Considering the location and the altitude of such a route, snow was liable to be a problem for several months a year. That was a difficult obstacle to overcome.

The second route would hug the southern border of the country. It would go from Atlanta, through Texas, and end in Southern California. There were mountains there, as well as deserts. The eastern end of that path also was a long way from the major markets of the Midwest and the East.

Then there was a central route, going right through the middle of the country. It could leave the Midwest, follow the Platte River in Nebraska and the South Pass in Wyoming, and head for California. The issue there was the Sierra Nevada, a mountain range that ran down the eastern side of California. From an engineering standpoint, building a railroad through that region would be a difficult job.

All of the possible routes and their variations had their supporters. Congress couldn't come close to picking one. While the debate continued, events in the West shaped the next step. A major silver deposit was found in Nevada in 1859, and Californians were anxious to mine the territory.

Judah Finds an Opening

Then an important discovery took place in 1860. Theodore Judah had built the first railroad west of the Missouri River when he built the Sacramento Valley line in 1856. Judah not only had a financial interest in a railroad that linked the country, but he also loved trains. Therefore, he jumped at the chance to explore what had become known as the Donner Pass in the Sierra Nevada range. Judah discovered that while most of the mountain range had two sets of peaks, making it very difficult for railroads to cross, the Donner Pass featured only one. Once past the high point going east, a route could be drawn along the Truckee River and into the great basin of Nevada. This solved the single biggest engineering hurdle to completing the central route.

Judah had always believed that business, not government, should play the lead role in construction. He got together with Sacramento businessman Collis Huntington, who eventually found other investors in Mark Hopkins, Charles Crocker, and Leland Stanford. They created the Central Pacific Railroad Company. Judah explored the Donner Pass again in 1861, when the situation in Congress changed dramatically.

Republican Abraham Lincoln took office in March 1861. By then, seven states making up the Deep South—South Carolina, Mississippi, Florida, Alabama, Georgia, Louisiana, and Texas—had left the Union. Virginia, Arkansas, North Carolina, and Tennessee soon followed. In between, the United States' Fort Sumter in South Carolina had been attacked by Confederate forces, marking the start of the Civil War.

This photo of construction of a railroad line near Donner's Summit in 1869 shows the difficulty of passing through the rugged terrain of the Sierra Nevada range.

The War Between the States played a large role in the creation of the proposed railroad. The Southern states were no longer a part of Congress, and therefore they could no longer block construction of a transcontinental railroad. The Northern states were free to pass such a law. That made it certain that the central route would be the one used for the project, which figured to bring population as well as political and economic power to the parts of the country it touched. Besides, the Northern states already had a well-connected grid of railroads in operation, something that would prove to be a huge help in winning the Civil War.

Judah spent the summer of 1861 working on a detailed map of the Donner Pass region of California. After completing it in the fall, he went to Washington, DC, to **lobby** for the railroad's adoption by Congress. He found

Railroad bridges, such as this one in 1863, frequently needed repairs in order to remain relatively safe.

an audience that was generally on his side. One important supporter was Lincoln himself. The Republican platform for the election of 1860, which sent Lincoln to the White House, stated:

> That a railroad to the Pacific Ocean is imperatively demanded by the interests of the whole country [and] that the Federal Government ought to render immediate and efficient aid in its construction; and that, as preliminary thereto, a daily overland Mail should be promptly established.

For the rest of 1861 and the first few months of 1862, discussion moved forward on the project. "I now conceive it my duty … to arouse this House from its inaction, and convince it … that this railroad is a necessity of the times," Congressman Aaron Sargent of California said.

Where to Begin

Arguments broke out about the starting points. Judah had lobbied successfully to begin construction near Sacramento, even at one point serving as the clerk to the House of Representatives' Pacific Railroad Committee. In that role, he actually wrote some of the legislation that eventually would authorize the railroad. A sticking point for the bill was where the beginning point of the project should be in the Midwest. The Mississippi and Missouri Railroad wanted to begin the tracks somewhere between Davenport and Council Bluffs in Iowa (west of Chicago). The Leavenworth, Pawnee and Western Railroad preferred to start in Leavenworth, Kansas (near Kansas City).

The House approved legislation to create the new railroad on May 6, 1862. In the Senate, two Iowa senators—James Harlan and James Grimes—threatened to kill the bill unless the starting point was designated for some place in Iowa. They won that argument; Council Bluffs was picked as the starting point. The Senate passed the bill on June 20.

That sent the legislation to President Lincoln, who signed the bill on July 1. The legislation said that this was "an Act to aid in the construction of a railroad and **telegraph** line from the Missouri river to the Pacific ocean, and to secure to the government the use of the same for postal, military and other purposes." The law also created the Union Pacific Railroad to handle the east-to-west portion of the railroad.

By any stretch of the imagination, this was a huge, costly project. The two companies were scheduled to receive government bonds to finance it. The Central Pacific and Union Pacific were to be paid $16,000 in bonds per mile built on a relatively flat grade of land, $32,000 per mile in the high portions of the plains, and $48,000 per mile in the mountains. Multiply that by 1,900 miles (3,058 km), and the money added up, particularly in 1862 dollars. A $16,000 payment

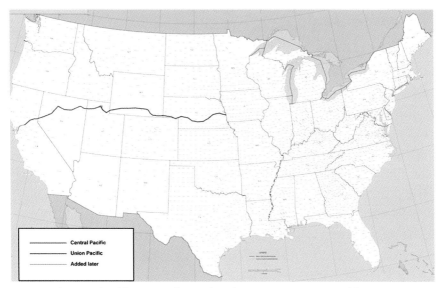

Train tracks were laid from Omaha, Nebraska, to Sacramento, California.

in that year would be worth about $381,000 today. Business leaders quickly figured out that there were big profits to be made in constructing such a railroad, and not just operating it.

In addition, the railroad companies were granted the **right-of-way** for 200 feet (61 m) on either side of the tracks. They also received 10 square miles (26 sq km) of land around the area of construction for each mile of track that was built. The companies were given until January 1, 1874, to complete the project, or the track and land would be returned to the government.

Who was in charge of this task? Two companies with little to no experience in railroads, and with virtual unknowns running them, had that assignment. Judah is said to have sent a telegram to the Central Pacific's office when the bill was signed: "We have drawn the elephant. Now let us see if we can harness him up."

"Done"

T he Union Pacific and Central Pacific railroad companies could not immediately start constructing the 1,900-mile (3,058 km) line across the United States right after President Lincoln signed the bill from Congress. Both companies had to assemble a workforce and collect raw materials. That would take some time.

However, the Central Pacific had some advantages because it wasn't starting from scratch. The California firm had a board of directors, and it had Theodore Judah. He was the most enthusiastic supporter of the idea in the country. In the Midwest, the Union Pacific appointed John Dix as its president and Thomas Durant as its vice president. Dix was hired mostly for his Washington connections. Durant was the man in charge.

Much of the attention for the new railroad was initially focused on the West. The eastern half of America was caught up in the Civil War, and it would be very difficult to acquire all of the materials needed during such a time. In January 1863, a giant groundbreaking ceremony was held in Sacramento. Leland Stanford, the new governor of California, threw the first shovel of dirt and a band played the song "Wait for the Wagon" as a joke. With that, construction was under way. Briefly. The next day, the *Sacramento Union* wrote:

> Underlying all the enthusiasm was a fear that it was a farce and not a fact which was being **inaugurated**.

Investors were nervous because the outcome of the Civil War was far from decided at that point, and no one was certain what the country might look like when—or if—the railroad was completed. These concerns made funding an issue. Tensions among the original investors in the Central Pacific grew in the summer of 1863. There were money problems, as the group did not have the personal funds to get the project going. Collis Huntington insisted that all of the investors immediately pay cash in exchange for stock. Judah didn't have that kind of money, and he also had the impression that the other board members were leaving him out of discussions about the future of the railroad. Judah's only hope of remaining involved was to find additional investors, and any possible candidates were in the East.

Judah took a boat to Panama in October as part of the voyage to New York, but he became sick during his time in the Central American country. His condition became worse by the time he arrived in New York City, and

Thomas Durant was the villain in the story of the railroad's construction.

he had to be carried off the ship to a hotel. Judah never recovered, and he died on November 2.

The Central Pacific put down the first rail of track in October 1863. It had some early success at laying tracks at the start, but the work just east of Sacramento was easy. Soon the hills of the Sierra Nevada arrived, and the pace slowed considerably. But it was fast compared to what was taking place almost 2,000 miles (3,200 km) to the east.

Dirty Dealing

The Union Pacific had a groundbreaking ceremony on December 2, 1863, in Omaha, Nebraska. Lincoln had ordered that the starting point be Council Bluffs, but Durant had moved it across the river to avoid paying for a bridge. Still, the new railroad hadn't really gotten started yet. Durant was too busy wheeling and dealing. He bought and sold **securities** in railroad lines that would tie into the transcontinental railroad before any announcements about those connections were made. He and his group made $5 million in the process.

Durant turned his attention to Washington. He spent about $435,000 of Union Pacific's money around Capitol Hill on congressmen in 1864 as he sought amendments to the 1862 bill. Durant was successful, and another law was passed. This time the railroads received even more land along the route, as well as the mineral rights, and limitations about an individual's ownership of shares in the railroads were dropped. It was a good deal for the railroad and its ownership, and a poor one for everyone else. The government also agreed to use the military to help the project by removing Native Americans from the planned route.

Durant wasn't done yet. He set up a new company, Crédit Mobilier of America, in October 1864. The company was created so that, in case of financial problems, the owners would only lose their own investment in the company. Their own personal fortune was not at risk, which was unusual at the time. Durant put a friend, Herbert Hoxie, in charge of Crédit Mobilier, and Hoxie submitted the only bid for construction of the rail line. It was approved by the board of directors. Essentially, Durant was paying himself to build the railroad without the threat of losses. Crédit Mobilier bought stock in Union Pacific at face value, but sold it to investors for less than it was worth. They made up the losses by overcharging the government for the costs of construction of the railroad.

Early in 1865, the fate of the transcontinental railroad seemed less than assured. Union Pacific still hadn't done much work in the Midwest, and Central Pacific was making little progress in the mountains of the West. In January 1865, President Abraham Lincoln asked Congressman Oakes Ames of Massachusetts to keep an eye on Union Pacific. Ames soon put money in Crédit Mobilier and lobbied other members of Congress on that company's behalf.

On April 9, 1865, the Civil War came to an end. Less than a week later, the nation paused to mourn the loss of Abraham Lincoln, who was assassinated by John Wilkes Booth. A train took Lincoln's body back to his home in Springfield, Illinois, for burial, and Grenville Dodge attended the service. "The sorrow was universal, for it was one of the greatest calamities of this or any other nation," he said later.

With the war over, Durant knew that the federal government would be able monitor the railroad more closely. He also knew that other rail companies were expanding to the western side of the Mississippi. He ordered construction to start in earnest that summer. Finally, the project got going.

Meanwhile, the Central Pacific started the difficult job of digging tunnels in the Donner Pass region of California. The area has some of the hardest rock in the world, and progress was at first measured in inches rather than feet or miles. The railroad hired Chinese workers in increasing numbers for the crew. They worked long days on those tunnels, either using picks and axes or explosive powder. It was a tough, dangerous job, and many workers were killed.

Portable Towns

Over the winter of 1865–1866, Union Pacific hired General Jack Casement to lead the construction effort. He set up transportable villages that could be packed up and moved down the railroad line as the miles were completed. These villages included places for the workers to eat and sleep. Other diversions, such as alcoholic beverages, were part of the baggage as well.

Author Samuel Bowles went along with the construction party, and described the scene in his book *Our New West*:

> These settlements were of the most perishable materials—canvas tents, plain board shanties, and turf-hovels—pulled down and sent forward for a new career, or deserted as worthless, at every grand movement of the Railroad company. Only a small proportion of their populations had aught to do with the road, or any legitimate occupation. Most were the hangers-on around the disbursements of such a gigantic work, catching the drippings from the feast in any and every form that it was possible to reach them. Restaurant and saloon keepers, gamblers, desperadoes of every grade, the vilest of men and of women made up this 'Hell on Wheels,' as it was most aptly termed.

The Union Pacific finally made good progress in 1866, heading west toward the Rockies. Newspapers published stories with **datelines** of "End of Track" as the work continued. But the Central Pacific was still stuck in the Sierra Nevada Mountains, its workers chiseling away. Science was about to provide a breakthrough to solve their problems.

Chinese workers set up camps along the construction route of the western portion of the railroad.

Nitroglycerin is an explosive made up of glycerol, and nitric and sulfuric acids. Ascanio Sobrero first made the substance in 1864. It was so unstable that he didn't want to see it used in public, but Sobrero couldn't keep the discovery a secret. In 1866, a small sample had blown up in San Francisco, killing fifteen people. Another nitroglycerin explosion took place on the railroad construction site, and six workers died. But the Central Pacific had seen the possibilities in the compound. When chemist James Howden walked into rail executive E. B. Crocker's office in the fall of 1867 and said he'd be willing to make the substance on site, thus avoiding a state ban on moving nitroglycerin. Howden was hired. The nitroglycerin was a huge step forward for construction. It

The Transcontinental Railroad

was more than 50 percent more effective than powder, and produced less smoke and other side effects.

There were hiccups along the way. Corporate infighting took place at the Union Pacific, as investor Oliver Ames (Congressman Oakes Ames's brother) jumped ahead of Durant to become the company president. Durant was furious and launched a flurry of legal actions that stopped construction for a while. Eventually, Durant regained his power, and work continued. Congressmen continued to ask Oakes Ames for the chance to buy into Crédit Mobilier at less than what it was worth; the company was paying out huge **dividends**.

Out West, Chinese workers staged a brief strike for higher wages. Central Pacific had been trying to hire workers at $35 per month, but the workers demanded $40 along with better working conditions. When their requests were turned down, they refused to work. "If there had been that number of white laborers … it would have been impossible to control them," Crocker said later. "But this strike of the Chinese was just like Sunday all along the work. These men stayed in their camps." After a week, hungry and discouraged, the workers agreed to go back to work at the same wages.

The Central Pacific reached an important milestone on August 27, 1867. It announced that it had finished drilling tunnels in the Sierra Nevadas. The achievement was almost matched a few months later when the Union Pacific's line went past the highest point on the entire route—8,200 feet (2,500 m) above sea level. "This summit I immediately named for my old commander, General [William Tecumseh] Sherman," said Grenville Dodge, who was now the project's chief engineer.

Meeting Up

Now it was simply a matter of reaching a meeting point. Both companies had relatively easy construction work

Chinese Workers

The Central Pacific needed workers to build its railroad line in the 1860s, but couldn't find any right away. The work was difficult and the pay was low, so few Americans were interested. By 1865, the railroad needed four thousand employees but only could find eight hundred.

What was the solution? Hire people who could find no other jobs. In California, that would be men of Chinese origin, who faced discrimination in their daily lives. Immigration from China to California started around 1850. The company started hiring large numbers of Chinese immigrants in 1865. Company executive Charles Crocker said of his new hires:

> Make Masons out of Chinamen? Did they not build the Chinese wall, the biggest piece of masonry in the world?

When the supply of immigrants ran out, workers were recruited from China. The new employees surprised many by becoming excellent workers. Eventually, 80 percent of the workforce was Chinese. "As a class they are quiet, peaceable, patient, industrious, and economical," Central Pacific president Leland Stanford said about them.

The contributions of the Chinese to the railroad have been remembered to this day: Chinese railroad workers were inducted into the Department of Labor's Hall of Honor in 2014.

This beautiful bridge on the Central Pacific route was built by Chinese laborers.

This bridge at Promontory Summit, Utah, was one of the last portions of the line to be completed.

ahead of them, and they were still paid by the mile. There were problems along the way—shortages of supplies and water, snow in the mountains, flooding on the plains, violent episodes with Native Americans, etc. Still, the railroad lines drew closer throughout 1868 and early 1869. There was only one catch left. The two companies had never gotten around to deciding where they would team up. With money to be made, the railroads kept building tracks. Soon Congress said enough, and ordered the two sides to figure out an end point.

They did, and couldn't have picked a more isolated spot. Promontory Summit is in northern Utah, not far from the Great Salt Lake. A ceremony was held on May 10, 1869, to mark the occasion of the joining of the two lines. Company and government officials, along with workers, crowded into the area to see the ceremonial driving of the final golden spike on the line.

For Men Only

If you could ask someone in the 1860s about the participation by women in the construction of the transcontinental railroad, the answer might sound like this: "This is no place for a woman."

There are few women who pop up in the story of the project. All of the construction laborers were men. For the Central Pacific, there are few mentions of women contributing to the railroad. It's possible that a few Chinese women worked in some way on the railroad.

To the east, a few of the managers of the Union Pacific did bring their families along. But the biggest presence of women probably came in the portable towns that were set up along the route. There was a need for cooks, seamstresses, and teachers along the way, and women filled those roles. In addition, these villages—which were torn down and moved up the tracks after a month —attracted all sorts of people who wished to join the workers in drinking, gambling, and other unsavory activities. Women were in that group.

A telegraph office had been built on the site for the occasion, and engines came up the tracks and parked nose to nose. Leland Stanford was given the honor of hitting the last spike. Alexander Toponce wrote down his memories from that scene:

> The first time he struck he missed the spike and hit the rail. What a howl went up! Irish, Chinese, Mexicans, and everybody yelled with delight. "He missed it. Yee." The engineers blew the whistles and rang their bells. Then Stanford tried it again and tapped the spike and the

The "Golden Spike" is hammered into the railroad tracks to complete the transcontinental railroad. This painting by Thomas Hill is titled *The Last Spike*.

telegraph operators had fixed their instruments so that the tap was reported in all the offices east and west, and set bells to tapping in hundreds of towns and cities … Then Vice President T. C. Durant of the Union Pacific took up the sledge and he missed the spike the first time. Then everybody slapped everybody else again and yelled, "He missed it too, yow!" It was a great occasion, everyone carried off souvenirs and there are enough splinters of the last tie in museums to make a good bonfire.

The news of Stanford's action was sent out in the form of a one-word telegram: "Done."

A single railroad now extended 690 miles to Sacramento to the west, and 1,086 miles to Omaha in the east. The transcontinental railroad had been finished.

Connected

In one sense, the completion of the transcontinental railroad in 1869 could be compared to the first landing on the moon in 1969. They were arguably the biggest projects of the century, and remain remarkable even today. The big difference is that we still don't know where the moon landing will lead us. The railroad's completion, however, had some obvious and almost immediate effects.

Let's start with the golden spike, which was quickly retrieved after the ceremony and shipped to California. It is on display at Stanford University. The area that was set up for the ceremony soon was taken apart. No one now knows exactly where the final spike was struck, but the National Park Service's site is at least in the neighborhood.

The two railroad companies then had to go back to work. They had been in such a hurry to get to the finish line that their workmanship wasn't first rate. So the Union Pacific and Central Pacific sent crews back along the route to make sure the rails were safe for passage. After that, the railroads were open for business. If you wanted to go from San Francisco to Omaha in 1869, the cost was $111 in first class. That's about $1,870 in today's dollars.

Two replicas of old-time railroad engines meet at the Golden Spike National Historic Site in Utah.

But it still wasn't possible to ride from the Atlantic to the Pacific by rail at that point. That milestone took more construction. At one end, the Central Pacific purchased the Western Pacific Railroad and completed a link between Sacramento and Oakland in November 1869. At the other end, the Union Pacific had plenty of trouble connecting the new rail line to the eastern half of the United States. The company's report to stockholders in 1871 said:

> The want of a bridge over the Missouri River, at Omaha to connect the eastern railroads with the Union Pacific, has been one of the most annoying incidents connected with the trip to California.

However, the Union Pacific Missouri River Bridge was completed in 1873, and Council Bluffs became a major transportation hub—as Abraham Lincoln predicted.

CENTRAL PACIFIC RAILROAD.

COMMENCING MAY 17, 1869, EX-
press Trains will run daily as follows:

EASTWARD.	Miles.	Time.
Leave Sacramento	—	6:39 A. M.
" Colfax	54	9:50 A. M.
" Truckee	120	2:10 P. M.
" Reno	154	4:20 P. M.
" Wadsworth	189	6:30 P. M.
" Winnemucca	324	1:45 A. M.
" Carlin	445	8:30 A. M.
" Elko	468	10:00 A. M.
" Toano	559	3:15 P. M.
Arrive at Promontory	690	11:05 P. M.

WESTWARD.	Miles.	Time.
Leave Promontory	—	6:15 P. M.
" Toano	131	3:00 A. M.
" Elko	222	8:25 A. M
" Carlin	245	9:35 A. M.
" Winnemucca	366	4:10 P. M.
" Wadsworth	501	12:05 A. M.
" Reno	536	2:10 A. M.
" Truckee	570	4:20 A. M.
" Colfax	636	9:50 A. M.
Arrive at Sacramento	690	1:20 P. M.

FARE.   Coin

Sacramento to Terminus.................$50 0
Children not over twelve (12) years of age
half fare; under five (5) years of age, free
100 pounds baggage (per passenger) free.

Two Trains daily (Sundays excepted) between Sacramento and Marysville, without
any change of cars:

Leave Sacramento at 6:30 A. M. and 2 P. M.
Arrive at Marysville at 9:30 A. M. and 5:30 P.M
Leave Marysville at 5:30 A. M. and 10:10 A.M.
Arrive at Sacramento at 9:45 A.M. and 1:20 P.M.

For tickets and other information, apply
at the Company's offices in Sacramento.

CHAS. CROCKER,
General Superintendent.
T. H. GOODMAN,
Gen'l. Passenger Agent.

The following are the present rates of fare
via UNION PACIFIC and connecting Roads:

Promontory to—	Currency.
Omaha	$81 50
St. Louis	101 50
Chicago	103 50
Cincinnati	114 85
Niagara Falls	118 90
New York	123 50
Boston	126 50

(Rates are subject to change.)

May 17, 1869.   265d&sw tf

UNION PACIFIC RAILROAD

THE GREAT
PLATTE VALLEY ROUTE

Is now complete and running daily passenger trains, forming in connection with
the Central Pacific Railroad an
ALL RAIL ROUTE TO CALIFORNIA
and the
PACIFIC COAST!
Through to San Francisco
In Less than Four Days!
Avoiding the dangers of the Sea.

Direct Connections made at
OMAHA
With Chicago and Northwestern, Chicago,
Rock Island and Pacific and St. Joseph and
Council Bluffs Railroads, and Missouri River
Line of Packets to and from all principal
Eastern and Southern Cities.

CHEYENNE,
With Stages for Denver, Central City,
Santa Fe, and points in Colorado and
New Mexico.

BRYAN,
With Stages for the great Sweetwater
Mining District.

UINTAH,
Stages leave on arrival of Union Pacific
trains for Salt Lake City and Southern
Utah.

CORINNE,
For Helena, Virginia City, and all points
in Montana.

PROMONTORY,
With Central Pacific Railroad for White
Pine Silver Mines, Sacramento, San
Francisco, and principal cities in Cali-
fornia, Nevada and Idaho.

First class Hotels and Eating Houses at
convenient points on the line.
Pullman's Palace and Sleeping Cars
accompany all trains.
For through rates on freight to Montana,
Sweetwater Mines and other points, apply to
H. BROWNSON,
General Freight Agent, Omaha.
C. G. HAMMOND,
Gen'l Sup't, Omaha,
J. BUDD, Gen'l Ticket Agent, Omaha.

A Salt Lake City newspaper published this advertisement detailing train schedules shortly after the railroad was completed.

The trip on the transcontinental railroad was not for the faint of heart, as this photograph of the track in Placer County, California, indicates.

Routes Expanded

Once one railroad across the country was built, others could follow on different routes. Rails connected San Francisco and Los Angeles in 1876, and then the tracks worked their way east. They crossed the Colorado River the next year, and reached El Paso, Texas, in 1881. It took two more years for the line to become a transcontinental railroad, with the route's completion coming in South Texas. This route had the advantage of being open throughout the year; snow in the Rockies sometimes closed the central route.

To the north, Congress in 1864 had chartered a new railroad to go from the Great Lakes to Puget Sound in Washington. Construction was slowed by the land's **topography**, and then stopped by an economic crash in 1873. No tracks were laid for years as the company

Birth of a Movement

Americans thought they had discovered an unlimited area of wilderness and resources when the transcontinental railroad opened up the West to settlement. They discovered in a short period of time that they were wrong. Scientists quickly found that we couldn't keep cutting down trees and damming rivers indefinitely; the effects of such actions on nature soon became evident.

Those who came to these unexplored lands quickly figured out that the natural beauty needed to be saved for future generations. President Ulysses S. Grant picked Yellowstone to be the first national park in 1872. Parks called Sequoia and Yosemite followed before the end of the century.

President Theodore Roosevelt, here shown speaking in Wyoming, was an important figure behind the regulation of land in the West.

In 1901, President Theodore Roosevelt changed government policy, which until that point had been to let people do whatever they wanted to the land. He put 230 million acres (93.1 million hectares) of land under federal protection, more than the combined total of his predecessors in that office. In a speech he made in Kansas on August 31, 1910, Roosevelt said:

> Of all the questions which can come before this nation, short of the actual preservation of its existence in a great war, there is none which compares in importance with the great central task of leaving this land even a better land for our descendant than it is for us.

The National Park Service was created in 1916. The conservation movement had been born.

dealt with bankruptcy. Finally, the route was finished on September 8, 1883.

That was three routes from east to west, and connecting routes between those railroads also were built. Travel was at first difficult, in part because life in the West still was a bit rough. Author Robert Louis Stevenson discovered that the usual rules didn't apply to parts of the West. He described riding the train there in 1879 this way: "They were speaking English all about me, but I knew I was in a foreign land."

The railroad grid in the western half of the country made it relatively easy for people to move to different sections. And move they did, in large numbers. In many cases they headed to the West Coast, in particular to California, with its mild weather and open spaces. But they also stopped along the way, and settled there, too. The population of the area west of the Mississippi by 1900 reached seventeen million. Between 1869 and 1900, Colorado, North Dakota, South Dakota, Montana, Washington, Idaho, Wyoming, and Utah became states.

The railroads themselves also grew. It didn't take long for all of the companies to agree on standards for the size of the rails, for example. That allowed trains to pass easily from one place to another. Railroads soon became the biggest users of wood and coal in the United States. Once the routes were established and connected, companies started to look for ways to provide better service for their customers. This led to the invention of devices such as automatic brakes.

Towns started to grow along the rail routes; you can still see the patterns on maps. All of those railroads crossing the country soon faced a large problem in their journeys. Each town had its own time based on the sunrise and sunset schedule. In other words, a traveler could go a handful miles west and his or her watch would not have a correct time. In 1883, four time zones were approved in the continental United States to solve that problem.

Starving the Opposition

Some villages grew into towns, and some towns grew into cities in places where hardly anyone had lived a few years earlier. The arrival of so many people into territory that had been virtually untouched for hundreds of years created complications. For example, herds of bison had been roaming across the Great Plains until the 1800s—some estimates put the number between thirty million and sixty million. The Native population had always relied on those animals as a source of food, clothing, and shelter, and defended them and their homeland with a fierce determination. There had been skirmishes between the white settlers and soldiers and the Native American population for several years, some of them quite savage on the part of both groups, but some treaties had been signed to allow travelers to pass through Native lands on their way west.

However, settlers kept coming, first on wagon trails and then in larger numbers on the railroad. The United States military came up with a plan. "Every buffalo dead is an Indian gone," said Colonel Richard Dodge in 1867. Five years later, Secretary of the Interior Columbus Delano wrote in his annual report:

> The rapid disappearance of game from the former hunting-grounds must operate largely in favor of our efforts to confine the Indians to smaller areas, and compel them to abandon their nomadic customs.

The Native Americans had little chance of defeating the American military. They had a few successes in the 1870s; their last major victory was Sitting Bull's rout of General

Hunters used the railroad to decimate bison populations in an effort to starve Native Americans. Telegraph lines run beside the tracks.

George Armstrong Custer's troops in Montana in 1876. Sitting Bull surrendered to American authorities about five years later. There were only brief skirmishes after that. About four hundred wild bison were left in 1893. Native Americans were often sent to reservations and told to adjust their lives to meet the laws and standards set by the United States government. It's a plan that never worked completely, and the Native population has been dealing with poverty and cultural issues ever since.

Scandal Exposed

On the money front, there was a price to be paid for the financial juggling done by Union Pacific and Crédit Mobilier. Union Pacific had earned $16.5 million on its part of the railroad, and that eventually caused suspicion. The *New York Sun* published a huge story on September 4, 1872, headlined "The King of Frauds—How the Credit Mobilier Bought Its Way Through Congress." The smaller headline read "Colossal Bribery— Congressmen Who Have Robbed the People, and Who Now Support the National Robber." Congress started to investigate later that year. Some of those who were said to have received stock were Vice President Schuyler Colfax, Speaker of the House James Blaine, future President James Garfield, and eleven

Vice President Schuyler Colfax's career was tainted by scandal.

others. Only two people in Congress, Oakes Ames and James Brooks, were punished by being **censured**. The rest suffered few consequences for their actions.

The villain in this part of the story probably is Thomas Durant, who started the scheme. He was fired by President Ulysses S. Grant in 1869. But Durant is said to have left with millions in his bank account. Justice needed four years to prevail in this case. Durant lost most of his fortune in the Crash of 1873. He spent most of his remaining years trying to fight lawsuits from angry former partners, and he died in 1885.

There were also problems in California. The four original partners in Central Pacific earned an estimated $40 million from the project, leaving the company with a massive debt that was left for communities and the federal government to pay.

It's easy to criticize the mistakes made in the construction of the transcontinental railroad from our viewpoint, 150 years after the fact. It's more important to remember how it affected lives from coast to coast.

Lines of Communication

A starting point is that telegraph lines were placed alongside of the tracks. That meant that the entire country had been connected on the original "information superhighway." Before the cross-country lines were installed, citizens often had to rely on spotty mail service to learn about national events. That process had been sped up considerably by telegraph reports. If additional details were needed, letters and newspapers now raced across the country on railroads.

Messages also could be sent involving financial transactions, meaning that the nation had been linked into one big market. That was important because the railroad made it much easier and cheaper for businesses to transport goods over long distances. Companies that served a large part of the country, if not the entire nation, were now possible. In 1880, freight worth $50 million was traveling across the country. European goods could reach the West Coast relatively easily, and the same was true for Asian goods headed for the East Coast.

Travel boomed. Business representatives could call on customers easily and expand their sales. People who became known as tourists were free to go anywhere in the country. Entertainers could present the same show from one coast to another, and never be heard in the same place twice.

The railroad also represented economic opportunity. For years, people had been tied to a specific plot of land, their business, or their job. When the railroad project was finished, they could easily pack up their possessions, take a train somewhere else, and start a new life. Historian George H. Douglas called it "a true Declaration of Independence."

Perhaps most important, the transcontinental railroad gave America a sense of unity. That feeling may have started around the Civil War. Historian Ken Burns points out that at the start of the Civil War, people would say "The United States are …" By the war's end, those same people would say "The United States is …" Now all of the citizens were mixing in ways that couldn't have been imagined at any previous time in American history.

America had been united. Abraham Lincoln's dream was finally complete.

Chronology

September 28, 1542: Juan Rodríguez Cabrillo "discovers" present-day California (although indigenous people had lived there for thousands of years). He claims the region for Spain.

April 30, 1803: The United States under President Thomas Jefferson buys 828,000 square miles (2.1 million square kilometers) of land west of the Mississippi River from France in a deal known as the Louisiana Purchase.

May 14, 1804: Meriwether Lewis and William Clark leave Camp DuBois with the Corps of Discovery to explore the Louisiana Purchase and try to find a water route to the Pacific coast.

July 25, 1814: George Stephenson's locomotive *Blucher* pulls 30 tons (27 metric tons) of coal up a 450-foot (137 m) incline in England.

March 3, 1820: The Missouri Compromise passes, excluding slavery in territories of the Louisiana Purchase north of latitude 36°30', except Missouri.

December 2, 1823: President James Monroe declares that the American continents "are henceforth not to be considered as subjects for future colonization by any European powers." This principle would become known as the Monroe Doctrine. Along with manifest destiny, it supplies support for westward expansion.

May 28, 1830: President Andrew Jackson signs the Indian Removal Act, allowing for the removal of Native Americans from their homelands in the East to unsettled land west of the Mississippi.

March 2, 1836: In the midst of a war with Mexico, Texas declares its independence from Mexico. The war ends with Texas becoming an independent territory. The issue of slavery delays its entry into the United States for nearly ten years.

May 22, 1843: A group of one thousand leaves from Independence, Missouri, by wagon train, heading over what would become known as the Oregon Trail to the Oregon Territory. A large-scale wave of westward migration follows.

January 28, 1845: Asa Whitney proposes to Congress the funding of a railroad to the Pacific Ocean.

July–August 1845: The term "manifest destiny" is coined by John L. O'Sullivan in an article on the annexation of Texas published in the *United States Magazine and Democratic Review*.

February 10, 1846: Members of the Church of Jesus Christ of Latter-Day Saints (Mormons) leave Illinois to escape persecution and head west for territory then controlled by Mexico. They settle in the valley of the Great Salt Lake in Utah.

April 25, 1846: The Mexican-American War, fought over the disputed border between Texas and Mexico, begins.

January 24, 1848: James Marshall discovers gold at John Sutter's mill in California. Marshall and Sutter attempt to keep the find secret.

February 2, 1848: Representatives from the United States and Mexico sign the Treaty of Guadalupe Hidalgo, ending the Mexican-American War and ceding more than 500,000 square miles (1.3 million sq km) to the United States.

September 9, 1850: California becomes the thirty-first state.

December 30, 1853: The United States buys 29,670 square miles (76,845 sq km) from Mexico in what is known as the Gadsden Purchase. The area later becomes part of Arizona and New Mexico.

May 30, 1854: Congress passes the Kansas-Nebraska Act, which overturns the Missouri Compromise and makes popular sovereignty the determining factor in allowing slavery to exist in a state.

July 1860: Theodore Judah finds a potential route for a railroad from California through the Sierra Nevada Mountains when he surveys the area around Donner Pass.

November 1860: The Central Pacific Railroad Company is created.

May 20, 1862: President Abraham Lincoln signs the Homestead Act, which provides settlers 160 acres (65 hectares) of public land west of the Mississippi provided they live on the land for five consecutive years. Opposition from proslavery groups had defeated previous efforts to pass such legislation.

July 1, 1862: Abraham Lincoln signs the Pacific Railway Act, which aids in the construction of the transcontinental railroad from Council Bluffs, Iowa, to the Pacific coast. The railroad is built between 1863 and 1869.

January 8, 1863: Governor Leland Stanford of California leads a groundbreaking ceremony for the new railroad line in Sacramento.

December 2, 1863: The Union Pacific breaks ground in Omaha, Nebraska.

July 1, 1864: Congress passes another railroad bill, which is even more generous to the railroads than the 1862 law was.

Spring 1865: Central Pacific begins digging tunnels through the Sierra Nevada Mountains.

July 10, 1865: The Union Pacific begins construction, spiking its first rail in Omaha.

October 6, 1866: Union Pacific lines cross the 100th meridian in Nebraska, giving the railroad the sole right to continue the line to the west.

August 28, 1867: Central Pacific workers finish blasting what comes to be known as Summit Tunnel.

November 30, 1867: Central Pacific directors celebrate the completion of the rail line to the eastern side of the Sierra Nevada.

April 16, 1868: Union Pacific crews reach the highest point on the route, Sherman Summit, at 8,200 feet (2,500 m), in Wyoming.

April 8, 1869: Railroad representatives meet in Washington and agree to have their lines meet north of the Great Salt Lake in Utah.

May 10, 1869: Workers join the Union Pacific and Central Pacific Railroads at Promontory Summit, Utah. Passengers can now travel from New York to California in just eight days.

September 4, 1872: A newspaper report breaks the news that corruption was involved in the construction of the transcontinental railroad.

March 25, 1873: The Union Pacific Missouri River Bridge is opened, making it possible to ride a train from New York to San Francisco.

June 25, 1876: Assembled tribes wipe out units of the Seventh Cavalry led by General George Custer at the Battle of Little Bighorn.

Glossary

abolitionist Someone who wanted to get rid of slavery.

buffer An area that prevents people or nations from coming into contact with each other.

censured An expression of severe disapproval, usually in a formal way, against an individual in Congress.

datelines Words at the start of a news story that tell where the event took place.

dividends Money paid out by companies to shareholders out of the company's profits.

emigrants People who moved from one part of a country to another region or to another country.

Great Plains A relatively flat grassland east of the Rocky Mountains that stretches from Canada to Texas.

inaugurated To start something or install a person into public office. It's often used in connection with the president of the United States.

Industrial Revolution The rapid development of industry due to the use of newly developed machines. It's often associated with Great Britain in the late 1700s and early 1800s.

lobby The act of trying to influence legislators to support proposed laws that will help selected organizations.

manifest destiny A popular belief during the 1800s that the United States should and would expand across the North American continent to the Pacific Ocean.

platform A formal set of goals, often published, that outlines the positions and philosophies of a particular political party or candidate.

reconnaissances Trips designed to gather and collect specific information.

right-of-way The right to travel on another person's property.

secede Withdraw from a federal union or political or religious organization.

security A piece of paper that has financial value and can be traded by individuals. It could be a stock, bond, or deed to land.

survey Examine a piece of land and use observations and measurements for such documents as a map or report.

telegraph A device used to send messages on a wire by making and breaking connections.

topography The arrangement of natural physical features, such as mountains and rivers, in a particular area.

tributary A river or stream that flows into a larger river.

Further Information

Books

Ambrose, Stephen E. *Nothing Like It in the World: The Men Who Built the Transcontinental Railroad 1863–1869.* New York: Simon & Schuster, 2000.

Bain, David Haward. *Empire Express: Building the First Transcontinental Railroad.* New York: Viking, 1999.

Borneman, Walter R. *Rival Rails: The Race to Build America's Greatest Transcontinental Railroad.* New York: Random House, 2010.

Cadbury, Deborah. *Dreams of Iron and Steel: Seven Wonders of the Nineteenth Century, from the Building of the London Sewers to the Panama Canal.* New York: Fourth Estate, 2003.

Douglas, George H. *All Aboard!: The Railroad in American Life.* New York: Paragon House, 1992.

Websites

Central Pacific Railroad Photographic History Museum

http://cprr.org

This website contains a massive amount of information on the transcontinental railroad, with 4,500 photographs included. It can be difficult to navigate but is fascinating to read.

Native American Tribes and US Government

http://www.victoriana.com/history/nativeamericans.html

The history of the Native Americans during the second half of the 1800s is a long, complicated story. This website provides a good overview of the subject.

PBS: Transcontinental Railroad

http://www.pbs.org/wgbh/americanexperience/films/tcrr

PBS has devoted a large amount of space to the railroad project, and it has a variety of links and other documents. The film itself is also worth your time.

Bibliography

Books

Ambrose, Stephen E. *Nothing Like It in the World: The Men Who Built the Transcontinental Railroad 1863–1869.* New York: Simon & Schuster, 2000.

Bain, David Haward. *Empire Express: Building the First Transcontinental Railroad.* New York: Viking, 1999.

Borneman, Walter R. *Rival Rails: The Race to Build America's Greatest Transcontinental Railroad.* New York: Random House, 2010.

Cadbury, Deborah. *Dreams of Iron and Steel: Seven Wonders of the Nineteenth Century, from the Building of the London Sewers to the Panama Canal.* New York: Fourth Estate, 2003.

Douglas, George H. *All Aboard!: The Railroad in American Life.* New York: Paragon House, 1992.

Solomon, Brian. *Union Pacific Railroad.* Osceola, WI: MBI Publishing, 2000.

Online Articles

"Asa Whitney (1791–1874) and Early Plans for a Transcontinental Railroad." PBS. Accessed September 5, 2016. http://www.pbs.org/wgbh/americanexperience/features/general-article/tcrr-whitney.

"Basic Facts About the Oregon Trail." Bureau of Land Management. Accessed September 5, 2016. http://www.blm.gov/or/oregontrail/history-basics.php.

Beard, Rick. "Working on the Railroad." *New York Times*, July 11, 2012. http://opinionator.blogs.nytimes. com/2012/07/11/working-on-the-railroad/?_r=0.

Bellis, Mary. "History of the Railroad: George Stephenson." About.com, February 3, 2016. http://inventors.about.com/ od/sstartinventors/a/Stephenson.htm.

"Building the Transcontinental Railroad." Library of Congress. Accessed September 7, 2016. http://www.loc. gov/teachers/classroommaterials/presentationsandactivities/ presentations/timeline/riseind/railroad/trans.html.

Central Pacific Railroad Photographic History Museum. Accessed on September 12, 2016. http://cprr.org/Museum/ FAQs.html.

"Chinese Immigration and the Transcontinental Railroad." United States Citizenship. Accessed August 30, 2016. https://www.uscitizenship.info/Chinese-immigration-and-the-Transcontinental-railroad.

"Completing the Transcontinental Railroad, 1869." EyeWitness to History.com. Accessed August 30, 2016. http://www.eyewitnesstohistory.com/goldenspike.htm.

"The Compromise of 1850." UShistory.org. Accessed September 14, 2016. http://www.ushistory.org/us/30d.asp.

"Comstock Lode." Online Nevada Encyclopedia. Accessed September 14, 2016. http://www.onlinenevada.org/articles/ comstock-lode.

"Historic Speeches: James Polk, 1848 State of the Union Address, December 5, 1848." PresidentialRhetoric. com. Accessed September 21, 2016. http://www. presidentialrhetoric.com/historicspeeches/polk/ stateoftheunion1848.html.

Jawort, Adrian. "Genocide by Other Means." *Indian Country Today*, May 9, 2011. http://indiancountrytodaymedianetwork.com/2011/05/09/genocide-other-means-us-army-slaughtered-buffalo-plains-indian-wars-30798.

"Original Journals of the Lewis and Clark Expedition, 1804–1806." W. W. Norton & Company. New York: Dodd, Mead, 1905. Accessed September 14, 2016. http://www.wwnorton.com/college/history/archive/resources/documents/ch09_03.htm.

Perry, Douglas. "The Lewis and Clark Expedition." National Archives. Accessed September 5, 2016. https://www.archives.gov/education/lessons/lewis-clark.

Rochester, Junius. "Oregon Territory, Establishment of." History Link, April 17, 2003. http://www.historylink.org/File/5446.

Smithsonian Magazine. "Lewis and Clark: The Journey Ends." *Smithsonian*, December 2005. http://www.smithsonianmag.com/history/lewis-and-clark-the-journey-ends-110100664/#GC5euHjOZRDbsOb6.99.

"Timeline: Transcontinental Railroad." PBS. Accessed September 6, 2016. http://www.pbs.org/wgbh/americanexperience/features/timeline/tcrr-timeline.

"Traveling on an Emigrant Train." EyeWitness to History.com. Accessed September 20, 2016. http://www.eyewitnesstohistory.com/emigranttrain.htm.

Index

Page and numbers in
boldface are illustrations.
Entries in **boldface** are
glossary terms.

About the Author

BUDD BAILEY has been a sports reporter and editor at the *Buffalo News* since 1993. Before that, he worked for the Buffalo Sabres hockey team and WEBR Radio. This is his seventh book, including four for Cavendish Square. Budd and his wife, Jody, live in Buffalo, New York. They love to travel throughout the United States, and have visited all fifty states. One of their stops was Promontory Summit, Utah.